THE RISE OF THE BLACK LIVES MATTER MOVEMENT

by Samantha S. Bell

BrightPoint Press

San Diego, CA

BrightP◇int Press

© 2021 BrightPoint Press
an imprint of ReferencePoint Press, Inc.
Printed in the United States

For more information, contact:
BrightPoint Press
PO Box 27779
San Diego, CA 92198
www.BrightPointPress.com

Content Consultant: Tani D. Sanchez, PhD, Professor, Africana Studies Program, University of Arizona

LIBRARY OF CONGRESS CATALOGING-IN-PUBLICATION DATA

Names: Bell, Samantha, author.
Title: The rise of the Black Lives Matter Movement / by Samantha S. Bell.
Description: San Diego, CA : BrightPoint Press, [2021] | Series: Understanding the Black
  Lives Matter Movement | Includes bibliographical references and index. | Audience:
  Grades 7-9
Identifiers: LCCN 2020047447 (print) | LCCN 2020047448 (ebook) | ISBN 9781678200664
  (hardcover) | ISBN 9781678200671 (ebook)
Subjects: LCSH: Black lives matter movement--History--Juvenile literature. | African
  Americans--Civil rights--Juvenile literature. | United States--Race relations--Juvenile
  literature. | Racial profiling in law enforcement--United States--Juvenile literature.
Classification: LCC E185.615 .B398 2021 (print) | LCC E185.615 (ebook) | DDC
  323.1196/073--dc23
LC record available at https://lccn.loc.gov/2020047447
LC ebook record available at https://lccn.loc.gov/2020047448

CONTENTS

AT A GLANCE

- The Black Lives Matter (BLM) movement started on social media. It began with a Facebook post and a hashtag.

- The movement began in 2013 after George Zimmerman was acquitted in the killing of Black teen Trayvon Martin.

- The movement grew in 2014 after a police officer killed eighteen-year-old Michael Brown.

- Protests grew as more unarmed Black individuals were killed by police. Protesters used slogans such as "No justice, no peace" and "I can't breathe."

- In May 2020, a Black man named George Floyd died after a Minneapolis police officer knelt on his neck for around eight minutes. Bystanders took video of the incident and posted it on the internet.

- Americans across the country reacted to Floyd's death by joining widespread BLM protests. Hundreds of thousands of people took to the streets demanding change.

- The BLM movement continued to be fueled through social media. Local chapters focused on what their communities needed.

- One of the movement's main goals is the shifting of funding from the police to other community programs. Organizers believe these programs are a better alternative to police involvement in many situations.

JUSTICE FOR TRAYVON

Black seventeen-year-old Trayvon Martin lived in Miami, Florida. In February 2012, he went to Sanford, Florida, to stay with his father for a few days. This city is near Orlando. His father's house was in a gated community. People were worried about robberies that had taken place in the area.

WE ARE ALL TRAYVON MARTIN

Images of Trayvon Martin would later become a common sight at protests.

George Zimmerman lived in the same neighborhood. He was part of the community watch program. People in the program watched for illegal activities.

Zimmerman often patrolled the streets in the neighborhood. He had a license to carry a gun.

On February 26, Trayvon walked to a convenience store to buy candy and a drink. Then he headed toward the house where he was staying. Zimmerman was driving down the road. He saw Trayvon walking on the sidewalk. He thought Trayvon looked suspicious, so he called the police.

The **dispatcher** told Zimmerman to stay in his car. But Zimmerman got out and followed Trayvon. Trayvon began running,

Sanford, Florida, became the center of national attention after the shooting of Trayvon Martin.

and Zimmerman caught up to him. Trayvon was unarmed. No one is sure exactly what happened next. Then Zimmerman shot Trayvon in the chest, and Trayvon died.

Zimmerman told the police he shot the teen in self-defense. He was not charged with any crime. Many people signed petitions demanding justice for Trayvon. Six weeks later, Zimmerman was arrested and charged with murder. On July 13, 2013, a jury found Zimmerman not guilty.

FROM PROTESTS TO A MOVEMENT

Many Black people were angry, especially young people. They could identify with Trayvon. Zimmerman thought Trayvon was a robber because he was young and Black. He was suspicious because of Trayvon's race. This is called racial profiling. Others had experienced racial profiling. People began protesting in the streets.

Protesters have spoken out about racial profiling and many other issues.

On the day of the verdict, a Black

activist named Alicia Garza wrote a post

on Facebook. In the post, she said, "Black

Patrisse Cullors was one of the activists who helped launch the Black Lives Matter movement.

people. I love you. I love us. Our lives matter."[1] Another activist named Patrisse Cullors saw the post. She added the hashtag #BlackLivesMatter.

The post was shared again and again. Soon Garza, Cullors, and another activist named Opal Tometi got together. They wanted to think of ways to fight violence against Black people. The movement they formed became known as Black Lives Matter (BLM).

CHAPTER ONE

HOW DID BLACK LIVES MATTER BEGIN?

During the next year, many incidents occurred between white police officers and Black citizens. One of them even involved a child younger than Trayvon Martin. People felt strongly that something had to change. The continuing incidents helped spur the early growth of BLM.

RALLY AT DEPARTMENT OF JUSTICE D.C.

ERIC GARNER

SON, FATHER, FRIEND, COMMUNITY MEMBER, HAD A RIGHT TO LIFE

Bus to rally: GarnerDOJRally.eventbrite.com

#PROSECUTEPANTALEO #BLMNY

BLACK LIVES MATTER NEW YORK

WE CANNOT

The Eric Garner case was a major event in the early days of the BLM movement.

DEADLY CONFRONTATIONS

On July 17, 2014, Eric Garner was in New York City. He was going to dinner with a friend. A fight broke out nearby, and Garner helped break it up. Police officers arrived and accused him of selling untaxed

cigarettes. When they tried to arrest him,
Garner argued with them. Officer Daniel
Pantaleo put him in a **choke hold**. Other
officers dragged Garner to the ground.
Garner had health problems. He said he
couldn't breathe. He died soon after.

"I CAN'T BREATHE"

Eric Garner's last words became a rallying cry
among protesters. In 2016, his siblings used
those words to write the song "I Can't Breathe."
The lyrics of the song reflect problems between
police officers and the black community.
Garner's sister, Ellisha Flagg, sang on the track.
His family said the song was "dedicated to the
struggle everyone is going through."

*Quoted in Daniel Kreps, "Eric Garner's Family Drops
Moving New Song 'I Can't Breathe,'" Rolling Stone,
July 11, 2016. www.rollingstone.com.*

On August 9, 2014, eighteen-year-old

Michael Brown and his friend walked

down the middle of the street in Ferguson,

Missouri. Officer Darren Wilson saw them.

He told them to move onto the sidewalk.

Brown and his friend refused. Wilson

stopped his car in front of them.

What happened next is still unclear.

Wilson said Brown came up to the

window of his police car. He said Brown

punched him and grabbed for Wilson's

gun. Then Brown ran away, turned back,

and acted like he was going to attack.

Some witnesses backed up Wilson's story.

Other people said Brown raised his hands in surrender. Some thought they heard Brown say, "Don't shoot." During the confrontation, Wilson shot Brown six times. Brown died on the street.

Tensions between black communities and largely white police forces were already

MAPPING POLICE VIOLENCE

After Brown's death, data scientist Samuel Sinyangwe helped create the website Mapping Police Violence. The website gathers information from various sources, such as social media, police reports, and obituaries. The site uses the information to produce data about police killings across the country. Sinyangwe explained that this website was meant to show Americans there was a national crisis.

high. Now people in the city reacted with rage. They were furious that the police had killed another unarmed Black man. They began protesting. A few began rioting. They **looted** stores and damaged businesses.

FROM MOMENT TO MOVEMENT

Soon the protests spread across the country. People wanted to take a stand for Michael Brown. They also wanted to stand for other Black Americans who had been killed by police. They chanted Brown's name and the phrase "Hands up, don't shoot." Investigators found no evidence that Brown had really said this. But it still became a powerful slogan. They also chanted, "Black lives matter." The hashtag had grown into a national movement.

BLM demanded changes in how police deal with people of color. People all over the country wanted to show their support. They started or joined local BLM groups, called chapters. Each chapter focused on the needs of its community. They took on different issues. Some chapters focused on education. Others focused on working with people who were abused. All of the chapters expressed the value of Black lives.

Activists listen to a speaker from a local chapter of BLM in Washington, DC.

The groups provided a network of support

for one another.

A FATAL MISTAKE

On November 22, 2014, twelve-year-old

Tamir Rice was at a park in Cleveland,

Ohio. He had a pellet gun with him.

Protesters would later hold Tamir Rice's photo at demonstrations.

He was pointing it at people. Someone called the police. They told the dispatcher that he might be a child and it looked like a toy gun. But the dispatcher did not tell the officers these details. The officers heard that there was a man with a gun. The officers shouted to Tamir to put down the gun. But within two seconds of arriving, Officer Timothy Loehmann shot the boy. He later said he thought Tamir was reaching for a gun. Tamir died.

Loehmann was still in training. He and his training officer gave statements about what happened. But what they said was not consistent. Neither officer was charged in Tamir's death. This decision led to more outrage and mass protests. The BLM movement gained even more momentum.

RISING ANGER

A few days later, on November 24, a **grand jury** made a decision in the Michael Brown case. The jury decided not to charge Wilson. Protesters took to the streets. Some of them reacted violently. Groups of people in Ferguson and nearby towns looted businesses. Many businesses were set on fire.

People around the country also showed their frustration. In New York City, demonstrators carried signs featuring the faces of Black Americans killed by police. Simone Gamble is a member of a group that observes police activity in New York. She stated, "The fight that's happening in Ferguson is happening here. We're going to

Police faced off against protesters as the situation in Ferguson became tense following the grand jury decision.

keep fighting and bringing attention to these issues until justice is served."[2]

Just over a week later, a grand jury made a decision in the Eric Garner case. The jury also decided not to charge the officers involved. Protesters returned to the streets. President Barack Obama said, "We are seeing too many instances where people just do not have confidence that folks are being treated fairly. . . . And it is incumbent upon all of us, as Americans, regardless of race, region, faith, that we recognize this is an American problem, and not just a Black problem or a brown problem or a Native American problem."[3]

Tamir Rice's case came before a grand jury in December 2015. The grand jury found that the officers had followed

The name of Tamir Rice would continue to appear at BLM protests for years to come.

procedure. They were not charged in

Tamir's death. BLM responded with

mostly peaceful protests. Later, the police

department found out Officer Loehmann

lied on his job application. He had not

People set up a memorial near the spot in the park where Tamir Rice was killed.

acted responsibly in his previous position. Loehmann was fired for this. But the community thought he should have been fired because of the killing. Cleveland city councilman Jeff Johnson said, "It's still a feeling that justice has not totally been done in this case. . . . It's like an open sore, and this is not going to help it fully."[4]

CHAPTER TWO

HOW DID THE MOVEMENT GROW SO QUICKLY?

Police violence against Black people has been a problem for a long time. US policing has roots in the slave patrols of the 1800s. These groups captured runaway enslaved Black people. The Civil War (1861–1865) ended slavery.

Inequality in policing helped drive the growth of the BLM movement.

Black Americans gained more legal rights throughout the 1900s. But discrimination continued. So did police violence. Black Americans are more likely to be killed by police than white Americans. A 2018 study found that the rate could be as much as 3.5 times higher.

MORE TRAGEDIES

Police violence has continued in the years since BLM started. More unarmed Black Americans have been killed. On April 4, 2015, Officer Michael Slager was on patrol in Charleston, South Carolina. He pulled over fifty-year-old Walter Scott for a broken taillight. But Scott was already in trouble with the law. He had not been paying **child support**. He jumped out of his car and ran.

Slager ran after him. Slager said Scott grabbed for Slager's Taser, so the officer fired his gun. But cell phone video told a different story. Scott was shot while running

Improvements in smartphone technology in the 2010s made it easier than ever to record and share video of police misconduct.

away. BLM held a peaceful rally. Slager was arrested and later convicted of murder.

The arrest of twenty-five-year-old Freddie Gray was also caught on video. Gray lived

Protesters marched in Baltimore after the death of Freddie Gray.

in Baltimore, Maryland. On April 12, 2015,

he was standing on a street corner. He saw

a police officer and started running. The

officers didn't know why he ran. They ran

after him and caught him. They said he was

carrying an illegal knife.

Gray was handcuffed and held down. He started screaming and said he couldn't breathe. But he didn't receive any medical help. Instead, officers put Gray in the back of a van and took him to the police station. He suffered severe injuries to his spine during the ride. He died a week later. Six officers were charged with crimes. Four of the officers were put on trial. But none of them were convicted.

On July 6, 2016, thirty-two-year-old Philando Castile was driving a car near St. Paul, Minnesota. His girlfriend and her four-year-old daughter were in the car too.

Officer Jeronimo Yanez pulled them over for a broken taillight. Castile did not try to run away. He did not complain. Castile had a registered gun in the car. He told the officer that he had one. When Castile reached for his driver's license, Yanez thought he was reaching for the gun. Yanez shot seven times into the car, killing Castile. Castile's girlfriend streamed a live video of the aftermath on Facebook.

Castile's mother urged protesters to remain peaceful. Yanez was charged in the killing. But in 2017, a jury found him not guilty. Thousands of people gathered

As time went on, more and more people of all races began to join BLM protests.

at Minnesota's state capitol. Protesters carried signs that said "Corrupt systems only corrupt" and "Unite for Philando." The protesters were mostly peaceful. Some walked onto the interstate, blocking it both ways.

Another tragedy happened in early 2020. Breonna Taylor was a twenty-six-year-old emergency medical technician in Louisville, Kentucky. Authorities believed her ex-boyfriend was involved in a drug ring. They thought he was having drugs delivered to her apartment. On the night of March 13, 2020, she was asleep at her apartment. Her current boyfriend, Kenneth Walker, was there too. The police knocked on the door. When they didn't hear an answer, they broke it down. Walker said he did not know who was breaking into the apartment. The officers were not wearing uniforms.

Walker legally owned a gun. He fired one bullet as a warning and hit an officer in the leg. The officers returned fire, shooting more than twenty times. Taylor was hit several times. She died in her apartment. After

"SAY HER NAME"

In September 2020, a grand jury made its decision in the Breonna Taylor case. It charged only one officer. These charges were for putting the neighbors in danger. No charges were brought against any other officers. After hearing the verdict, protesters across the United States took to the streets. They demonstrated against police brutality and racial injustice, chanting, "Say her name." This slogan called attention to Black women harmed by police brutality whose stories are often overlooked.

Taylor was killed, one officer was fired for blindly shooting in the apartment building. Months later, that officer was charged with endangering people in nearby apartments. New York congresswoman Alexandria Ocasio-Cortez later said about Taylor, "We know that her death is not just the result of one person but the system, structure, and department that failed their entire community."[5]

THIS TIME IS DIFFERENT

On May 25, 2020, forty-six-year-old George Floyd was arrested in Minneapolis, Minnesota. Police believed he used a fake

People set up a large memorial at the spot where Floyd was arrested.

twenty-dollar bill in a grocery store. They

handcuffed Floyd and tried to put him in

a police car. Floyd resisted entering the

car. He said he was afraid of enclosed

spaces. Floyd fell to the ground. Officer Derek Chauvin knelt on his neck. Two other officers pinned down Floyd's back and knees. A fourth officer kept the crowds away.

Floyd was on the ground for around eight minutes. He told the officers that he could not breathe more than a dozen times. He told them that he was dying. Then he stopped moving and breathing. An ambulance took Floyd to the hospital. He was pronounced dead there. **Bystanders** caught the incident on video and posted it online.

KEY PLACES

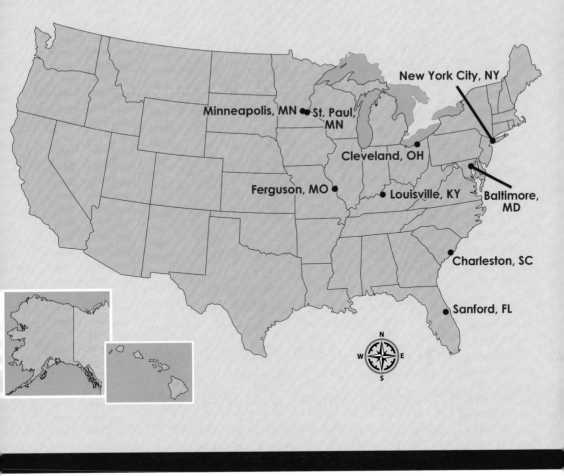

High-profile incidents of violence against Black people have happened in a variety of different cities across the country.

PROTESTS IN A PANDEMIC

During this time, Americans were dealing

with the COVID-19 pandemic. The disease

had spread rapidly throughout the world. Local governments asked people to stay at home. Doing so would slow the spread. People across the country read about George Floyd's death. Millions of people watched the video of his arrest.

Americans of all races began to feel the trauma of Floyd's death. Normal life had already been disrupted due to the pandemic. Many public places were closed because of the virus. People could not go to restaurants or movie theaters. They could not go on vacation. Now the feelings of sadness and anger in the wake of Floyd's

Face coverings became a common sight at protests during the COVID-19 pandemic.

death helped connect people around

the country.

Scholars suggested these factors led

to more Americans supporting the BLM

movement. They put signs in their yards.

They posted "Black Lives Matter" on

Yard signs were one way people showed their support for the ongoing protest movement.

social media. Hundreds of thousands of people started using hashtags such as #GeorgeFloyd, #BlackLivesMatter, and #ICantBreathe. By mid-June 2020, as many as 21 million adults had participated in BLM protests. This made it the biggest protest movement in US history.

WORLDWIDE IMPACT

George Floyd's death did not just impact Americans. People in many countries were affected. After he died, protests and memorials took place around the world. People everywhere wanted to honor Floyd as well as other victims of racism. Flowers and notes were left at memorials across Europe, Africa, Asia, Australia, and South America.

CHAPTER THREE

HOW HAVE AMERICANS RESPONDED?

The BLM movement expanded following Floyd's death. Suddenly, people of all ages and races wanted to join. They wanted to support justice and equality. They were angry about what happened to Floyd. They were also frustrated that there were still many racial issues in America.

BLM protests grew larger than ever before in the summer of 2020.

The day after Floyd died, people

started protesting in Minneapolis. They

gathered outside a police station. They

condemned racism and demanded justice

for Floyd. They also called for an end to

police brutality. Some of the protesters began damaging the police station. The officers used **tear gas** to regain control.

The next day, people in Los Angeles, California, began protesting too. The protesters chanted, "No justice, no peace." They also repeated, "I can't breathe." Within a few days, the protests had spread to other large cities. These included New York City; Atlanta, Georgia; and Washington, DC.

Over the summer, millions of Americans joined in the protests. More than 10,000 demonstrations took place between late May and the end of August. About 7,750 of

The message of BLM spread to protests in other countries, including the United Kingdom.

these were linked to the BLM movement.

The protests were held in more than

2,000 different locations. Sociology

professor Kenneth Andrews explained,

"The geographic spread of protest is

a really important characteristic and

helps signal the depth and breadth of a

movement's support."[6]

BLM did not lead every protest. But the

local chapters provided materials for people

MODERN-DAY FREEDOM RIDERS

By 1961, the US government had outlawed segregated bus stations. But few bus stations in the South changed their policies. Black and white activists from across the country traveled to the South to help desegregate stations. They became known as Freedom Riders. After the death of George Floyd, cyclists in Rochester, New York, formed the ROC Freedom Riders. They use bicycles to carry the message of racial justice. They chant and protest as they ride through Rochester.

who wanted to get involved. Activists shared information about the protests on social media. That way, protests could take place all across the country.

PEACE TURNS TO VIOLENCE

Most of the protests were peaceful. But in more than 500 of the protests, some people became violent. The protests turned into riots. Protesters broke into stores and looted them. They set buildings and cars on fire. They destroyed businesses. Some people causing damage were not BLM supporters. They were trying to make protesters look bad.

In some of these riots, innocent people were killed. These included Black seventy-seven-year-old David Dorn. He was a retired police captain. During one of the riots in St. Louis, Missouri, he went to check on his friend's pawn shop. He was killed protecting the store. Chris Beaty was a Black thirty-eight-year-old former university football player. He was shot and killed during a riot in Indiana.

Many people began protesting in Portland, Oregon, too. But the peaceful demonstrations soon became violent riots. The riots took place on more than

Most BLM protesters were peaceful, but fires, property damage, and violence happened at some protests.

100 nights during the summer of 2020.

Protesters **vandalized** stores and

restaurants. They set fires and threw rocks.

They robbed and beat people in the streets.

The federal government sent federal police into the city in July. Critics said that the federal officers increased the violence.

POLICE-FREE ZONES

On June 8, 2020, protesters moved into a neighborhood in Seattle, Washington. They created the Capitol Hill Autonomous Zone (CHAZ). It was later renamed the Capitol Hill Organized Protest (CHOP). It covered six blocks. It was to be a peaceful, police-free community. Things seemed to go well at first. People could get free food and medical supplies. They planted gardens. But within three weeks, it had become a dangerous area. There were multiple shootings, and two Black teenagers were killed. The police shut CHOP down.

NO MORE MONUMENTS TO SLAVERY

The focus of the protests expanded beyond police violence. Protesters also started vandalizing statues and monuments that had a connection to slavery. These objects glorified the actions of racist people. Some were marked with graffiti or broken. Others were taken down altogether.

Christopher Columbus has often been described as a hero who discovered America. But he and his men had enslaved some of the indigenous peoples of the Americas. Protesters tore down statues of Columbus due to this history. One of

In the summer of 2020, work crews took down some statues connected to slavery.

the statues was in Baltimore. A crowd of

protesters yanked down the statue and

pushed it into the harbor.

It is against the law for people to remove or damage public statues. Some cities took steps to remove statues legally. Some were moved to museums. Others were placed in storage. Still others were moved to private property. To many people, the statues symbolized racism. They believed the statues had to be removed for the country to move forward.

LESS POLICING, MORE COMMUNITY

The main focus of BLM is stopping police violence against the Black community. The movement called for cities to defund the police. This meant that a city would take back some of the money that went to the police department. The money would then be used for community services. For example, money might be used to hire social workers, improve education, or fight poverty. Activists believed these steps could help prevent crime. Fewer police would be needed.

Political leaders in several large cities agreed. These included Los Angeles; Austin, Texas; and Baltimore. The mayor of New York City promised to cut the budget of the police department by $1 billion.

Defunding the police became a popular BLM message.

CHAPTER FOUR

WHAT IS THE FUTURE OF BLM?

BLM began with a hashtag. Social media helped the movement spread around the world. Anyone could show their support by posting #BlackLivesMatter.

After Floyd's death, more people did this than ever before. From July 2013 through May 2018, the hashtag was used nearly 30 million times on Twitter. This was an

Social media made it easy to spread the word about protests across the globe.

average of 17,002 times per day. But after

the death of George Floyd, it spread even

faster. From May 26, 2020, to June 7,

2020, the hashtag was used approximately

47.8 million times on Twitter. This was an

average of about 3.7 million times per day.

Large corporations used social media to show support too. These included Ben & Jerry's, Netflix, and Nike. One Reebok tweet said, "Without the Black community, Reebok would not exist. America would not exist. We are not asking you to buy our shoes. We're asking you to walk in someone else's. To stand in solidarity. To find our common ground of humanity."[7]

OPPOSITION TO THE MOVEMENT

Yet not all Americans support the BLM movement. This does not always mean they do not care about these issues. Most Americans agree that police violence

Some corporations, including the ice cream company Ben & Jerry's, came out strongly in support of BLM.

against Black people must stop. But

some do not agree with the policies

BLM supports.

One BLM goal is to defund the police.

Supporters believe community programs

would do more to reduce crime. However, many Americans are not in favor of this. In September 2020, Michigan voters were surveyed. About 75 percent opposed defunding the police. Only 18 percent supported the idea.

However, part of the issue may be confusion. Not everyone understands what defunding the police means. They may think it means getting rid of the police entirely. In the same Michigan survey, 58 percent of people said they supported BLM. And 57 percent said they supported shifting some police funding to social services.

Police reform became a divisive issue even as support for BLM rose.

Some people believe the defunding

slogan has cost BLM some support.

Political consultant Mario Morrow explained,

"When you take it too far with a message

that does not resonate with all the people

Violence at protests was usually rare, but some people associated this destruction with the BLM movement.

who are now supporting you, then you start losing your support base."[8]

Many people also oppose the violence that emerged at some protests. Most protesters were peaceful. However, a few turned violent. Bystanders posted videos of the violence online. The looting and

"ALL LIVES MATTER"

Some people who oppose the BLM movement use the phrase "All Lives Matter." It may sound like this phrase values every individual. Yet for many people, saying "All Lives Matter" is distracting and harmful. It takes the focus off of the Black community. BLM wants people to understand the unique dangers Black people face.

destruction caused the movement to lose some support.

LOOKING AHEAD

The protests of 2020 carried the message of BLM further than ever before. Not everyone supported the movement. But they could agree that it had a major effect on the country. BLM forced Americans to talk about racial issues. The next step was to find solutions.

BLM leaders are excited about the movement's growth. They see it continuing to change the country. BLM has become a voice for unheard people.

The collected voices of millions of individuals helped drive the BLM message forward in 2020 and beyond.

Giant protests in the summer of 2020 helped make BLM one of the biggest protest movements ever.

BLM founder Alicia Garza says, "We've connected people across the country working to end the various forms of injustice impacting our people. We've created space for the celebration and humanization of Black lives."[9]

THE BREATHE ACT

In July 2020, BLM organizers introduced the BREATHE Act. It would get rid of some police programs. It would move money to community-led programs. People would have less contact with the police. But before the BREATHE Act could become a law, it would have to be approved by Congress and signed by the president.

GLOSSARY

activist

a person who campaigns for political or social change

bystanders

people who watch an event but do not take part in it

child support

court-ordered payments to support one's minor children

choke hold

a tight grip around a person's neck that restrains the person by restricting his or her breathing

dispatcher

a person who receives emergency calls and organizes the response of emergency services

grand jury

a group of citizens that decides whether criminal charges should be brought against someone

looted

stole goods from a business during widespread upheaval

tear gas

gas used to force crowds to disperse

vandalized

destroyed or damaged on purpose

SOURCE NOTES

INTRODUCTION: JUSTICE FOR TRAYVON

1. Quoted in Marie-Christine Ghreichi and Sara Osman, "BLM and Social Justice," *U of Minnesota*, July 28, 2016. https://cla.umn.edu.

CHAPTER ONE: HOW DID BLACK LIVES MATTER BEGIN?

2. Quoted in Nicholas St. Fleur, "Scenes from a Ferguson Protest in New York City," *Atlantic*, November 25, 2014. www.theatlantic.com.

3. Quoted in Tanya Somanader, "Statement on the Grand Jury Decision in the Death of Eric Garner," *Obama White House*, December 3, 2014. https://obamawhitehouse.archives.gov.

4. Quoted in Melissa Etehad, "Cleveland Policeman Who Shot Tamir Rice Is Fired," *LA Times*, May 30, 2017. www.latimes.com.

CHAPTER TWO: HOW DID THE MOVEMENT GROW SO QUICKLY?

5. Quoted in Josh Wood, "Breonna Taylor," *Guardian*, September 23, 2020. www.theguardian.com.

CHAPTER THREE: HOW HAVE AMERICANS RESPONDED?

6. Quoted in "Demonstrations and Political Violence in America," *ACLED*, September 30, 2020. https://acleddata.com.

CHAPTER FOUR: WHAT IS THE FUTURE OF BLM?

7. "Reebok," *Twitter*, May 30, 2020. www.twitter.com/reebok.

8. Quoted in Melissa Burke, "Michigan Voters Back Black Lives Matter," *Detroit News*, September 9, 2020. www.detroitnews.com.

9. Alicia Garza, "A Herstory of the #BlackLivesMatter Movement by Alicia Garza," *Feminist Wire*, October 7, 2014. www.thefeministwire.com.

FOR FURTHER RESEARCH

BOOKS

Eric Braun, *The Civil Rights Movement*. Minneapolis, MN: Lerner, 2019.

Clara MacCarald, *Rage and Protests Across the Country*. San Diego, CA: ReferencePoint, 2021.

Rachel L. Thomas, *#BlackLivesMatter: Protesting Racism*. Minneapolis, MN: Abdo, 2020.

INTERNET SOURCES

Catilin Abber, "These Teens and 20-Somethings Are Organizing the Civil Rights Movement That Will Change Our Country," *MTV.com*, December 19, 2014. www.mtv.com.

Gene Demby, "How the Recent Black Lives Matter Movement Gained Increased White Support," *NPR*, June 17, 2020. www.npr.org.

"Trayvon Martin Shooting Fast Facts," *CNN*, October 19, 2020. www.cnn.com.

WEBSITES

African American Museum in Philadelphia
www.aampmuseum.org

The African American Museum in Philadelphia, Pennsylvania, houses and interprets the work of African Americans.

Black Lives Matter
www.blacklivesmatter.com

The official website of Black Lives Matter features information about the movement and its goals.

National Museum of African American History and Culture
https://nmaahc.si.edu

The National Museum of African American History and Culture features information about Black history, including the protest movements of the past and present.

INDEX

IMAGE CREDITS

ABOUT THE AUTHOR

Samantha Bell lives in the foothills of the Blue Ridge Mountains. She has written more than one hundred nonfiction books for kids on topics ranging from penguins to tractors to surviving on a deserted island.